# 1 MONTH OF
# FREE
# READING

## at

## www.ForgottenBooks.com

---

By purchasing this book you are eligible for one month membership to ForgottenBooks.com, giving you unlimited access to our entire collection of over 1,000,000 titles via our web site and mobile apps.

To claim your free month visit:
www.forgottenbooks.com/free204590

ISBN 978-0-484-38385-1
PIBN 10204590

# MAGPIES
# IN PICARDY

By
T. P. CAMERON WILSON

LONDON:                    1919
THE POETRY BOOKSHOP
35 DEVONSHIRE STREET,
THEOBALD'S ROAD, W.C. 1

*(Published May 15th, 1919.)*

6045
2 M 3

PRINTED IN ENGLAND BY
THE WESTMINSTER PRESS, 411A HARROW ROAD

# Contents

# THE SENTIMENTAL SCHOOLMASTER

# Introduction

THE Author of the following poems was killed in France, in early manhood, on March 23rd, 1918. The selection here printed represents the best of his verse, none of which has hitherto been published, except in newspapers and periodicals.

In August, 1914, he enlisted in the Grenadier Guards. Subsequently he was commissioned in the Sherwood Foresters, in which regiment he served for a long period overseas. At the time of his death he was a captain, and, according to all accounts, an energetic and experienced soldier.

His friends, however, will wish to remember him as a writer of clear promise and a great companion ; while the boys who worked under him, as a schoolmaster, will feel, all their lives, the benefit of his influence. He had the power, in an unusual degree, of becoming the comrade of his pupils, and of making their existence happy and their education a natural enjoyment.

His literary talent showed itself precociously early, but afterwards developed rather slowly. He was extremely shy about his verse, and, unlike most youthful poets, was always disinclined to let it be

# INTRODUCTION

seen, or discussed, by his friends. During, however, the last year or two of his life, there was a certain expansion, a power to enjoy the fact that the ideas he was expressing had some definite emotional value. He would soon (if there are *might-have-beens*) have developed an individual mode and rhythm which could have placed him among the most original poets of the time.

Those who may wish to know more of him should read his one novel, " The Friendly Enemy," or his letters from France, which will some time be published. His prose is, in certain cases, stronger and more finished than his verse. To readers of the *Saturday Westminster* he was well known as " Tipuca," and, on his death, in that paper, at least, there was unanimous expression of regret for the loss of a valued contributor.

The question whether the poems which follow are, or are not, important contributions to the literature of our time will be decided by their readers. As the expression of a personality they are, at any rate, remarkable. Earthly promise is not for the dead. But the image of it is to be loved. If their author did not reach his full literary strength, it was only because he was not allowed to live long enough.

These words are written, so far as possible, in such a spirit of impartiality as he would have preferred. He sought no praise. It would be doing him an injustice to attempt, on account of his fine life

# INTRODUCTION

and patriotic death, to inflate the merits of his poetry. For these reasons an introduction to it is only possible, if brief. It will be the function of the editor of his letters and other prose remains to narrate, and attach these to, the events of his life.

H. M.

# Acknowledgment

The following poems previously appeared in *The Westminster Gazette* :—Magpies in Picardy ; During the Bombardment ; Sportsmen in Paradise ; St. John vii, 6 ; Under the Frosty Stars ; Time's Fool ; Farmhouse ; Piskies ; Heaven. An Old Boot in a Ditch was first printed in *The English Review* ; A Funeral at Princetown in *Poetry and Drama* ; and the series entitled " The Sentimental Schoolmaster " in *T.P's. Magazine*.

# MAGPIES IN PICARDY

THE magpies in Picardy
 Are more than I can tell.
They flicker down the dusty roads
And cast a magic spell
On the men who march through Picardy,
Through Picardy to hell.

(The blackbird flies with panic,
The swallow goes like light,
The finches move like ladies,
The owl floats by at night ;
But the great and flashing magpie
He flies as artists might.)

A magpie in Picardy
Told me secret things—
Of the music in white feathers,
And the sunlight that sings
And dances in deep shadows—
He told me with his wings.

(The hawk is cruel and rigid,
He watches from a height ;
The rook is slow and sombre,
The robin loves to fight ;
But the great and flashing magpie
He flies as lovers might.)

He told me that in Picardy,
An age ago or more,
While all his fathers still were eggs,
These dusty highways bore
Brown singing soldiers marching out
Through Picardy to war.

# SONG OF AMIENS

LORD ! How we laughed in Amiens !
For here were lights, and good French drink,
And Marie smiled at everyone,
And Madeleine's new blouse was pink,
And Petite Jeanne (who always runs)
Served us so charmingly, I think
That we forgot the unsleeping guns.

Lord ! How we laughed in Amiens !
Till through the talk there flashed the name
Of some great man we left behind.
And then a sudden silence came,
And even Petite Jeanne (who runs)
Stood still to hear, with eyes aflame,
The distant mutter of the guns.

Ah ! How we laughed in Amiens !
For there were useless things to buy,
Simply because Irène, who served,
Had happy laughter in her eye ;
And Yvonne, bringing sticky buns,
Cared nothing that the eastern sky
Was lit with flashes from the guns.

And still we laughed in Amiens,
As dead men laughed a week ago.
What cared we if in Delville Wood
The splintered trees saw hell below ?
We cared . . . We cared . . . But laughter runs
The cleanest stream a man may know
To rinse him from the taint of guns.

# DURING THE BOMBARDMENT

WHAT did we know of birds ?
　Though the wet woods rang with their blessing,
And the trees were awake and aware with wings,
And the little secrets of mirth, that have no words,
Made even the brambles chuckle, like baby things
Who find their toes too funny for any expressing.

What did we know of flowers ?
Though the fields were gay with their flaming
Poppies, like joy itself, burning the young green
　　maize,
And spreading their crinkled petals after the showers—
Cornflower vicing with mustard ; and all the three
　　of them shaming
The tired old world with its careful browns and
　　greys.

What did we know of summer,
The larks, and the dusty clover,
And the little furry things that were busy and starry-
　　eyed ?
Each of us wore his brave disguise, like a mummer,
Hoping that no one saw, when the shells came over,
The little boy who was funking—somewhere inside !

# SPORTSMEN IN PARADISE

THEY left the fury of the fight,
  And they were very tired.
The gates of Heaven were open, quite
Unguarded, and unwired.
There was no sound of any gun ;
The land was still and green :
Wide hills lay silent in the sun,
Blue valleys slept between.

They saw far off a little wood
Stand up against the sky.
Knee-deep in grass a great tree stood . . .
Some lazy cows went by . . .
There were some rooks sailed overhead—
And once a church-bell pealed.
" God ! but it's England," someone said,
" And there's a cricket field ! "

# A SOLDIER

HE laughed. His blue eyes searched the morning,
Found the unceasing song of the lark
In a brown twinkle of wings, far out.
Great clouds, like galleons, sailed the distance.
The young spring day had slipped the cloak of dark
And stood up straight and naked with a shout.
Through the green wheat, like laughing schoolboys,
Tumbled the yellow mustard flowers, uncheck'd.
The wet earth reeked and smoked in the sun . . .
He thought of the waking farm in England.
The deep thatch of the roof—all shadow-fleck'd—
The clank of pails at the pump . . . the day begun.
" After the war . . . " he thought. His heart beat
     faster
With a new love for things familiar and plain.
The Spring leaned down and whispered to him low
Of a slim, brown-throated woman he had kissed . . .
He saw, in sons that were himself again,
The only immortality that man may know.

And then a sound grew out of the morning,
And a shell came, moving a destined way,
Thin and swift and lustful, making its moan.
A moment his brave white body knew the Spring,
The next, it lay
In a red ruin of blood and guts and bone.

    .    .    .    .    .    .    .    .    .

Oh ! nothing was tortured there ! Nothing could
     know
How death blasphemed all men and their high birth
With his obscenities. Already moved,
Within those shattered tissues, that dim force,
Which is the ancient alchemy of Earth,

Changing him to the very flowers he loved.

.    .    .    .    .    .    .    .    .

" Nothing was tortured there ! " Oh, pretty thought !
*When God Himself might well bow down His head*
*And hide His haunted eyes before the dead.*

# ON LEAVE
## (To R. H. and V. H. L. D.)

IT was not the white cliff at the rim of the sea,
Nor Folkestone, with its roofs all bless'd with
    smoke ;
Nor the shrill English children at the quay ;
Not even the railway-bank alight with primrose
    fire,
Nor the little fields of Kent, and the woods, and
    the far church spire—
It was not these that spoke.

It was the red earth of Devon that called to me,
" *So you'm back, you li'l boy that us used to know !* "
It was the deep, dim lanes that wind to the sea,
And the Devon streams that turn and twist and run,
And the Devon hills that stretch themselves in the
    sun,
Like drowsy green cats watching the world below.

There were herons stalked the salty pools that day,
Where the sea comes laughing up to the very rails. . .
At Newton I saw Dartmoor far away.
By Paignton there was one I saw who ploughed,
With the red dust round him like a sunset cloud,
And beyond in the bay was Brixham with her sails.

How could I fail to mourn for you, the brave,
Who loved these things a little year before ?
In each unshattered field I saw a grave,
And through the unceasing music of the sea
The scream of shells came back, came back to me.
It was a green peace that suddenly taught me war.

Out of the fight you found the shorter way
To those great silences where men may sleep.
We follow by the paths of every day,
Blind as God made us, hoping that the end
May hear that laughter between friend and friend
Such as through death the greater-hearted keep.

We are not weary yet.  The fight draws out,
And sometimes we have sickened at the kill,
And sometimes in the night comes slinking doubt
To whisper that peace cometh not through Hell.
But yet we want to hear God's anger tell
The guns to cease their fury and be still.

We are not weary yet, though here the rain
Beats without shame upon the shattered dead.
And there I see the lazy waves again.
And in the weedy pools along the beach
The brown-legged boys, with their dear Devon
    speech,
Are happier than the gay gulls overhead.

Up the wet sand a spaniel sputters by,
Soused like a seal, and laughing at their feet ;
There is a gull comes slanting down the sky,
Kisses the sea, and mews, and flies away.
And, like flat jewels set against the grey,
The roofs of Brixham glitter through the heat.

It was for this you died : this, through the earth,
Peace and the great men peace shall make,
And dogs and children and careless mirth . . ..
Beauty be with you now—and of this land
In bloody travail for the world you planned,
God give you deep oblivion when you wake.

# AN OLD BOOT IN A DITCH

THERE is an epic of the winding path
 That might be sung by you—
Mornings when Earth came glowing from her bath
And shook her drowsy laughter into dew,
And little ways your younger brothers made
Went up the hills and danced into the blue.

Noons when the great sun hammered out a blade
Upon the silent anvil of the downs,
And in divine inconsequence you strayed
Over the hill kings, with their bramble-crowns
And saw, across the meadow-patterned plain,
The far still smoke of little valley towns.

And evenings, when the Earth gave thanks for rain,
And all the washen soil of her did seem
Sweeter than little children who have lain
All night among the roses of a dream ;
And great white clouds went up the stairs of God
And gnats danced out above the misty stream.

Yet most, I think, the broad high road you trod
Would weave its marching splendour with your
          song—
The weariness that held the feet you shod,
The weariness that makes all roads too long,
Until the spirit trails its beaten wings
And finds the whole earth given to the strong,

And all the thousand crushed and broken things
Whose hope has snapped beneath the feet of Gold
Peer upward through the dust His passing flings
And see Him watch the hopeless road unfold—

Staring across the passion at His feet
With yellow eyes that glitter, and are cold.

It is not so, but when our spirits meet
Old Weariness, with his rust-eaten knife,
There is no corner of our house kept sweet
That is not trampled bloody by the strife,
Until with hungry fingers he lays bare
A rawness hidden in the quick of life.

It is not so. In your green silence there
You see the world pass like a lean old witch,
You watch the stars at night, and you may share
That small, fierce love wherein the soil is rich,
And know that half the gifts of God are won
By centipedes and fairies in the ditch.

# THE MAD OWL

STAY near me, oh ! stay near me in the dark !
The Fear is crawling in the shadows now,
The old vague fear thou speakest of as mad . . .
Stay near me while we hunt.  I catch again
That swift wild glimpse beneath the staring moon,
Of something owl-like in the very soil—
As though the rotten wood-reek of the earth,
The ravenous weeds, the life-betraying grass,
(All the strange stuff of the soil) were quick
With that same living that our feathers know.
Stay near me, oh ! stay near me as we hunt,
I almost fear the field mouse when he screams,
Because his shrill, thin tenor speaks to me
Of life that is as ours.  I watch the earth,
I watch the small food stirring in the grass,
And cannot fall in silent death to it,
Because it seems as some wild brotherhood
Had caught my wings and held them from the kill.
Oh, listen !  I have even dared to doubt
That God was all an owl. . . . I have seen Him
Without a beak, without his silent wings . . .
Speaking another voice . . . nor calling wide
Over the dim earth with that mellow scream
Such as we know He hunts with. . . .

# A FUNERAL AT PRINCETOWN
## (*Written in* 1912.)

IT was a bleak road from the gaol, was the road
    we trod,
Tugging at something heavy under the slanted rain.
And the moor there was twisted and scarred with
    pain,
Like a tear-stained face, staring defiance at God.

It was the father walked in front, and he read in a
    book
With little Latin words flung under grieving skies,
And the warders there with death asleep in their
    eyes,
And the Mother of Churches little beneath their
    look.

And we dropped him into the little clean-cut hole
That smelled of rain, and the clay whereof we are
    made,
And one of us laughed, and one of us shouldered a
    spade,
And one of us spat, while the father prayed for his
    soul.

And the mist over the moor, crawling and dim,
Was blind like the great beast Man with his thousand
    necks
Who mouths through a gloom of laws, nor ever recks
Of a dead face, staring defiance at him.

# STANZAS WRITTEN OUTSIDE A FRIED-FISH SHOP

O MOTHER Earth! Whose sweetest visions move
Through the blue night in silver nakedness,
What awful laughter mingled with your love
That here my sense should feel the wild caress
Of knowledge breaking common walls of sight
To see the hills march cloudward and grow less?

Here is no splendour of the wistful night
Staring wide-eyed beneath the stars' disdain.
Only a fallen sister of their light
Offers her beauty to the careless rain.
Only between the houses in the dark
Is something of your loneliness—and pain.

Yet here you told my senses to embark
And sail the seas whose smallest isle is Space,
To touch far beaches near the Sun, and mark
Baby Eternity under Heaven's face;
And lo! the wind that bent my sunlit sail
Was this foul fish-breath from a cursed place!

I saw men stirring while the dawn was pale—
A low green ribbon in the waking east—
I heard the waters beating with their flail,
And felt the hate that links unto the beast
All soulless things of yours when Man is near,
Lusting to make your rebel son their feast.

I saw the stubborn face men set to fear,
The dogs of toil that gnawed their bleeding hands;
I saw brine-sodden ropes slip through and sear

Their frozen fingers as with white-hot brands.
I saw them face the hardness of all hells
That men might eat dead things in foreign lands.

Deep in the green and silver mass that swells
The dripping nets of those who find fate good.
I saw the awful war of hidden cells,
The dim primæval tissues seeking food ;
And all their armies, mouthing through the gloom,
Called to their kinsmen in the fishers' blood.

I saw all History and her pageant-doom,
Mocking to-day with an eternal mirth,
While the old threads were twisted on your loom,
The fraying threads of life and death and birth :
Their woof a moment rough beneath my hand,
As though I dared to test the weaver's worth;

As though a moment in the fickle sand
I saw the steps of Fate go up the beach,
And some vague purpose in this plan unplanned
Leapt into sight—yea almost into speech,
Before the evil reek that brought it me
Swept it again with laughter out of reach.

# THE SUICIDE

## (*August Bank Holiday*.)

THERE must be some wild comedy in Hell,
  For men will laugh because their souls have died
And beauty is become a silly shell
With old, decaying, sexual jests inside.
They laugh aloud, although their eyes have seen
The passionate beauty of the broken spray,
The stealthy shadows creeping through the green,
The footprints of the wind when he is gay.
They look upon the sea with her desire—
Like a green woman, hungry though she sleeps,
While her swift dreams, on pinions of white fire,
Call with the gulls above her slumbering deep . . .
They laugh, they laugh, and throw things every-
    where—
Stones at the sea, at bottles in the sand
("You see that bloody gull, Bill, over there ?
Well, watch me hit him, here from where I stand.")
O God ! what ugly fools we are l
I will stand up and strip these clothes away—
One real white body shining like a star
Out of the coloured dark of their array—
Give myself fiercely to the sea's embrace,
Sink on her bed nor let my life arise ;
Feel her salt lips upon my drownèd face.
Her eyes . . . the growing greenness of her eyes !
Then when the empty white shell that was I
Shall float again within their affrighted reach
The laughter in their thousand throats will die
And they will hear the waves along the beach,
Hear the curv'd waves in broken song unroll'd,
And look a moment at the eternal sea
In wonder at the triumph my eyes have told.
For wisdom will be whispered unto me,

The wisdom that may not be said with words,
Which little fishes know who swim the deep,
And rabbits in the hedge, and little birds,
And little children smiling in their sleep.

THE troubled dust,
   Torn from the stolid world ;
Sleepless as lust,
   Rain-sodden, tempest-hurled ;
Hating its lowly birth,
   And beating ghost wings to arise
From its scornful mother, the Earth,
   To the laughter of watching skies . . .
He wrote in it—God who knew
   The dreary sickness of things,
The straining to reach the blue
   With broken and bloody wings. . . .

Did He (even He) grope in a sudden dark,
And scrawl in the dust—a question mark ?

# UNDER THE FROSTY STARS

UNDER the frosty stars I flung my window
    wide ;
Saw in the farmhouse yard the common farmhouse
    things
Deep-drowned in the silver sea of the moon's full
    tide,
(To and fro on its hinge my leaded casement swings,
Wide to the airs of heaven like an elfin door,
While away and away from beneath sweeps the moor.)

Moorland and hill were closed in a silver smear,
Sprinkled with sparks where the homesteads of
    Bovey lay,
And the good familiar things of the farm stood clear,
With their hard black shadows cutting against the
    grey.
I dreamed of them, sleepless under the frosty skies
Like old tried sentinels, watching with friendly eyes.

But the morning came, slow-footed and strangely
    calm,
With a dimly-shrouded brilliance of drowsy light.
My sleep-brimmed eyes from the window leapt to
    the farm,
And behold his forehead was diademed with white,
And the friendly farm things there in the yard below
Raised faces transfigured with shining masks of snow.

# KNIGHT-ERRANT

WHEN I put on my morning tie
    The souls of ladies come to me;
Their faces through a mist I spy
    Like silver drown'd in a green sea.

And all about their necks I find
    (Their necks, like children's, sweet and white)
Dim colours that they take and bind
    About my arm before the fight.

But never while the daylight runs
    Does shadowy armour break the grey.
Only a gleam of foreign suns
    Strikes a veiled sword, and dies away.

Only behind the walls of sense
    Some magic laughter breaks its chain
And like a bird, with pinions tense,
    Hovers . . . then falls to flight again.

# THE INN

MY soul is an Inn whose guest is God.
　　All this dark, dusty, winding stair
Into the silent sunlit room He trod,
　　And He is there.

Hush ! the great door is locked and barred :
　　Only He and I have the key.
See you the prayers that stand on guard,
　　Watching for me ?

Within, when the casement opens wide,
　　The room is filled with the sound and scent
Of the world without, in a sunlit tide
　　By Him unpent.

The breath of newly-watered soil,
　　And of pine trees in a summer sun.
The songs of reapers brown with toil,
　　When work is done.

The murmur of a sleepy sea ;
　　The prayers of children at God's feet ;
The humming of a drowsy bee
　　In noonday heat.

And down from the window sweeps from view
　　An orchard with apples shadow-kissed,
And a meadowed valley dim and blue
　　With early mist.

And the Autumn red of brackened hills ;
　　And the blue-green of a windy sea ;
And a swaying flame of daffodils
　　Beneath each tree.

And bluebells gleaming through the fern ;
  And silent, shadow-freckled lanes ;
And gaunt, lone uplands bleak and stern,
  Lashed with wild rains.


And white foam flung where breakers boom,
  And sea caves where the green floor swings :
Thus in the silence of the room
  I see all things.


Ah ! but the Inn has other guests,
  Who lie sleep-flushed and drunk with life,
Slinking forth when the dim world rests,
  For cunning strife.


Through the dusty ways and shadowed turns
  They creep to the great locked door,
And deep and foul is the lust that burns
  Each heart for war.


And sometimes in the outer court
  Foul nettles grow and tangled weeds,
And twisting creeper-strands of thought,
  Whose flowers are deeds.


They clamber up the crumbling walls
  And clutch and claw the stonework grey,
Till faintly through the casement falls
  The shrouded day.


And sometimes wild and thunderous gales
  Beat madly from the outer night,
And through the dusky Inn there wails
  A scream of fright.

And sometimes I have forced my way
    In drunken madness when He calls,
And bid Him—I ! no longer stay
    Within these walls.

My soul is an Inn whose guest is God,
    Yet, ah ! He stays for love alone,
So squalid are the rooms He trod,
    So mean His own !

# DEAR, IF YOUR BLINDED EYES . . .

DEAR, if your blinded eyes could see
The paths my thoughts have worn to you,
The trodden roads from you to me,
I wonder, would some sweet surprise,
Or scorn, make dim those sunlit eyes,
As winds, beneath a tent of blue,
Make dusk the gold with passing feet
Silently over the laughing wheat.

# TIME'S FOOL

MEMORY, Memory calls to me
　　Out of a faded day,
Over the tides of a silver sea
　　Rain-dimmed into silent grey.

" When the nursery fire," says Memory,
　　" Made drunken giants at night,
And you were a little pink dumpity-dee
　　Burrowing out of sight,

" You whispered low to your friendly bed,
　　' I'll kill 'em in herds and flocks
When I am a growed-up man ' (you said)
　　' And keep their bloods in a box.'

" But you always dreamed," says Memory,
　　" That the hills you were going to climb
Were builded by bland Eternity
　　And not by feverish Time.

" When your punt was moored," says Memory,
　　" By the willow-mirrored Cher,
And you heard dim sounds of energy
　　From the blazing parks afar,

" There were shadowy giants that you saw,
　　And their slaughter was still your plan,
For under your tilted, sun-freckled straw
　　Your whisper was : ' Now I'm a man.'

" But you always dreamed," says Memory,
　　" That the hills you were going to climb
Were builded by bland Eternity
　　And not by feverish Time."

# THE DEAD MARCH IN "SAUL"

A MELODY of birth,
  A cry of little life,
Torn from the sons of Earth,
And faint with weariness of unfulfilling strife
Beats its frail hands against the wings of Death.
Vast and invisible are they, throbbing the troubled
    air
With storm-pulsed waves of thundered ecstasy.
And yet a breath,
Fainter than laughter of dead jests is there.

As when in Spring beneath a rainy soil
The dead things stir and move toward the sun,
So from the deeps of unproductive toil
Moves the faint breath of something that was done,
So faint, so little, that to those that sweat
To wrench achievement from the iron of thought,
There comes a knowledge (and their eyes are wet)
Of eagle-wings by trailing cobwebs caught.

And then,
Riving the heart of things,
Crashes the laughter of Death,
Poising on thunderous wings,
" Little my fools," he saith,
" Ye that have given me hate,
And loathing and bitter fear,
He whom ye mourn at the gate
Laughs with me here."

# CAPTAIN OATES

WE lifted up our eyes,
    Up from the multitudinous trouble of the sands
That fringe the quieter trouble of Time's sea,
And saw, behind the centuries, old calm gods arise
To whom our fathers raised undoubting hands—
Saw them arise, yet could not bow the knee.

Ours was a wisdom which was somehow sad,
Sad with the knowledge that divinity was dead,
Or that our sight was grown too clear to mark
God's builded wall between the good and bad.
With shattered certainties our temple steps are red:
We wait, to hear His laughter through the dark.

Yet here the old divinity broke through,
The old dumb heroism strove,
Towering in mountainous silence over pain,
The old proud scorn of death's dramatic due,
The fear of such eternal words as *love*.—

    .    .    .    .    .    .    .    "

We nod him greeting.  Then to work again.

# THE FEAR OF GOD

THEY worshipped God, and all about them flung
  A beauty of blue smoke, and down far aisles
The fainting gold of lamps was hung.
They worshipped God with heart and tongue.

As little rabbits run when men pass by,
And crouch wide-eyed beneath the scented sod,
So all that dim world turned to fly
When past the pillars rang a cry.

God's friendly right hand to the roof he reared,
His laugh shot all the smoky dusk with sun :
They ran when God Himself appeared,
For God was naked, and they feared.

# FARMHOUSE

THE white wall, the cob wall, about my Devon
farm.
The oak door, the black door, that opens to the
wold.
Down the grey flagstones, and out in the gloaming,
(And all across my shoulder her milk-splashed arm.)
Out in the cool dusk to watch the rooks homing.
(And all across the grey floor a slant of gold.)

The oak door, the black door, that opens to the
skies.
The dim hall, the grey hall, when all the work is
done.
Where the great bolt is our hands make a meeting ;
(And all across my laughter her love-lit eyes.)
There at the closed door we hear our hearts beat-
ing.
(And all across the red west a fiery sun.)

The dim hall, the grey hall, wherein our soul is
guest.
The black door, the dread door, that opens to the
night.
Down the worn flagstones our two lives together.
(And all across our wonder, whispers of rest.)
Out from the firelight to face windy weather.
(And all across the rain-clouds a dawning light.)

# PISKIES

*(Writ in Devon.)*

THERE'S piskies up to Dartymoor,
  An'tidden gude yew zay there bain't.
I've felt 'em grawpin' at my heart,
I've heard their voices callin' faint,
I've knawed a man be cruec down—
His soul fair stogged an' heavy-like—
Climb up to brawken Zaddle Tor
An' bare his head vor winds to strike.
An' all the gert black mawky griefs,
An' all the pain an' vog an' grime,
Have blawed away and left en clear
Like vuzz-bush vires in swalin' time.
An' what med do so brave a thing
As thic' white spells to tak an' weave,
But li'l piskies' vitty hands,
Or God Himself as give 'em leave ?
But tidden Him would stop an' spy
From Widdicombe to Cranmer Pule,
To maze the schemin' li'l heart
Of every Jacky-Lantern fule !
For mebbe 'tis a lonesome rod
Or heather blooth, or peaty ling,
Or nobbut just a rainy combe—
The spell that meks 'ee tek an' sing.
An' this I knaw, the li'l tods
Be ever callin' silver faint.
There's piskies up to Dartymoor,
An' tidden gude yew zay there bain't.

# FRANCE, 1917

INTO the meadows of heaven one of the great
    dead came
As a man comes home to the old boy-haunted hills.
The little hills of heaven climb
From the green sea, and smell of mint and thyme.
And he found the whole land gay with the blue that
    fills
Evening and cups of hare-bells and young eyes
And the glooms and hollows of Autumn where wood-
    smoke lies.


The great dead greeted him with a schoolboy shout,
" You have been long from the hills of heaven,"
    they said,
" And you reek of Space, and the things that may
    never be small,
The vast, cold fields that reach in vain for a wall,
The plains where never a cloud gets overhead,
And the hells without horizon . . .
                                    Get you clean
In the little brooks of heaven, that run through
    friendly green."


He said, " I have passed through the fringe of space,
Where the lit worlds lie like fallen fruit in the grass;
And, passing, I saw in the dusk a world apart.
Like a remembered friend it caught my heart,
Held me, and would not let me pass,
Saying, ' I am the Earth. You must remember me :
The clouds are mine, and woods, and the restive
    sea.' "

38

Like starlight came a wonder to their eyes.
" Of all worlds I have loved it best," said one.
" I know a holy city. . . ."
                              " There were towns . . ."
" There was a dog that loved me . . ."
                              " Do the downs
Still, with their lazy roads and hawthorns, sleep in
    the sun ? "
" I made a garden. . . . . After Summer showers
Moths swam like ghosts above the drenchèd flowers."


He said, " I saw the cloud-shadow of the land
Lie on the green sea, ragged with cape and bay.
And I saw the dark of woods that were spilled like
    wine ;
Spires and white roads and a river's silver line,
And beaten leaves of gold where the cornfields lay.
There were two sails like linnets—swift and brown,
Making the harbour of a little town.


The port was sprinkled dark with moving men,
Whose thoughts above their toil flashed in the blue,
Swift and more beautiful than dragon-flies . . .
Up from a lonely church I saw arise
The prayers of women—fiercer than they knew,
Full of the fear which great love makes too strong ;
Half-threatening God to save their men from wrong.


The quays were heaped with all the stuff of war ;
Not the gay colours that laugh to Eastern suns,
No spices and spill'd cloths of purple and milk,
No blue and cinnamon bales of scented silk,
But the grim iron and the great beast-snouted guns,
And oil-engines passing with their loads
Of white unpainted wood that smelled of forest
    roads.

39

And round them slept the cornfields in the sun.
I passed great roads straight as a strong man's prayer,
Villages drowning in the blue of trees,
Gardens whose colour seemed to sing with bees.
Courage and hope and bitter love were there,
And I saw proud sorrow lie like a mist of the soil
About the women of France at their stubborn toil.

Very lonely they seemed—the women of France ;
And the children, holding in leash the giant Earth,
Like insects on the vast, indifferent lands,
Yet changing the face of the soil with their careful
     hands.
Nature might watch them with a contemptuous
     mirth,
But the fields were rich with food as I went by,
And the gathered shocks stood shaggy against the
     sky.

On every road War spilled her hurried men,
And I saw their courage, young and eagle strong.
They were sick for home—for far-off valley or moor,
For the little fields and lanes, and the lamp-red
     door ;
For the lit town and the traffic's husky song.
Great love I saw, though these men feared the name
And hid their greatness as a kind of shame.

Man makes a town as God makes man himself,
Not suddenly, but adding cell to cell,
Till through the never-finished clay upsprings
The reluctant beauty of familiar things.
A dead town and the body's broken shell
Are for the night to cover and earth to hide . . .
There were wooden crosses there, by a town's
     pierced side."

Nothing was in the graves but the stuff of flowers.
I saw gay daffodils there, awaiting birth.
And over them, like a cloak on children asleep,
The love of all the women who hope or weep.
There were wounds here in the green flesh of the
      earth ;
The hungry weeds had come to their own in the
      corn,
And even the beauty of trees was raped and torn.

The guns were there in the green and wounded
      wild,
Hurling death as a boy may throw a stone.
And the man who served them, with unquickened
      breath,
Dealt, like a grocer, with their pounds of death.
Thunderous over the fields their iron was thrown,
And beyond the horizon men who could laugh and
      feel
Lay in the wet dust, red from brow to heel.

The bodies of men lay down in the dark of the
      earth :
Young flesh, through which life shines a friendly
      flame,
Was crumbled green in the fingers of decay. . . .
Among the last year's oats and thistles lay
A forgotten boy, who hid as though in shame
A face that the rats had eaten. . . . Thistle seeds
Danced daintily above the rebel weeds.

Old wire crept through the grass there like a snake,
Orange-red in the sunlight, cruel as lust.
And a dead hand groped up blindly from the mould. . .
A dandelion flamed through ribs—like a heart of
      gold,

And a stink of rotten flesh came up from the dust . . .
With a twinkle of little wings against the sun
A lark praised God for all that he had done.

There was nothing here that moved but a lonely
    bird,
And the wind over the grass.  Men lived in mud ;
Slept as their dead must sleep, walled in with clay,
Yet staring out across the unpitying day,
Staring hard-eyed like hawks that hope for blood.
The still land was a witch who held her breath,
And with a lidless eye kept watch for death.

I found honour here at last on the Earth, where
    man faced man ;
It reached up like a lily from the filth and flies,
It grew from war as a lily from manure.
Out of the dark it burst—undaunted, sure,
As the crocus, insolent under slaty skies,
Strikes a green sword-blade through the stubborn
    mould,
And throws in the teeth of Winter its challenge of
    gold."

# THE SENTIMENTAL SCHOOLMASTER

## TO AN EXCEEDING SMALL NEW BOY

O! LITTLE and untutored, we have won!
    In shadow-glamoured deeps you caught our
      words,
In silent spaces freckled with the sun
    And sweet with love, and hushed with wings of
      birds.

You raised bright eyes and, like all little things
    That play about the feet of laughing gods,
You dressed our speech with swift imaginings
    Of giant engines moving giant rods.

And like all little things that sleep and wake
    Held close with starry silences, as with an arm,
You shrank from ice-brained fools who reached to
      take
    Your frightened mind from haunts all mother-
      warm.

What bait of ours has won them from your side
    To play the traitor and forget your due?
The Swimming-bath? Our Colours in their pride?
    Our titled Parent? Or our Soccer Blue?

For lo, O! little cub, you are dragged forth!
    And all your hushed retreats are far away,
And fairies wring their silver hands in wrath,
    And bow their heads and weep for you to-day.

They know that in a month you will unlearn
 The thousand laughing melodies of Pan,
And unto such as me for guidance turn,
 And I—my God !—what am I but a man ?

# TO THE SCHOOL RADICAL

THEY moved in that unhallowed corridor
  (Whence to my study come far sounds of war) ;
And through a broken net of sound there beat
The song of your defeat.

Olympian scorn to which your name gave birth
Had touched you with its little stings of mirth,
And though (I learned) your heart is brave to fight,
You sob, sometimes, at night.

Could not the great blunt fingers of the Day
Push back the guards that held your tears in sway,
And yet Night kiss them from their stubborn line,
O little friend of mine ?

From whose rough-welded faith have you unslipp'd
A badge of such small honour that it stripp'd
Your soul of careless friendships, and the joys
That are belov'd of boys ?

Does he, to-night—the sire whose creed you own—
Think of the splendid sorrow he has sown ?
Are any (save the fool that teaches you)
Praying as fathers do ?

# THE MATHEMATICAL MASTER TO
## HIS DULLEST PUPIL

I CAME to you and caught your eagle wings
And gloomed your soul with Algebra and things,
And cast a net of pale Geometry
Wherein your laughter struggled to be free.

They say that mental discipline is grand
For teaching little striplings how to stand.
They say I cannot fit your soul for life
Without continual pruning with a knife.

And they are clever men, who come from schools
Where they were made successful by these rules,
And where they gained that weight of flesh and bone,
Which I would give my oldest pipe to own.

And so they must be right and I be wrong,
Yet when I see sweet thoughts around you throng
Like honey-bees above the tousled gorge
In smoke-blue valleys under Devon tors,

And when, O little son ! within your eyes
The light that lives on wings of dragon-flies
(More delicate than laughter of dead jests)
Is drowned beneath your pedagogue's requests,

I go and swear and smoke and drink
And dream of vested interests, and think
Of all the poets' fire we might have won
Had you and I been pals, O little son !

# TO HIS BLACKBOARD

O! YOU whose eyes inscrutable have known
    The tortured sons of learning in this room,
And noted blandly from your tripod-throne
    Their grapplings with a hydra-headed gloom ;

Give me some tithe of your tranquillity,
    Of that calm scorn wherewith your soul is filled,
That, even as you, I may but coldly see
    Bleak wisdom taught and understanding killed.

And, even as you, stare Sphinx-like into space,
    Nor march the chalky floor all tousle-haired,
When bright boys mention with a cheerful face
    That $(a + a)$ is written down $a^2$.

Nor turn my face fierce-eyed towards the stars,
    And bite my reeking pipe-stem till it snaps,
To think of all the hopes a pedant mars,—
    The wingèd dreams that die within his traps.

# TO A BOY WHO READ POETRY FOR
## HIS PLEASURE

WHAT would your courtly father say ?—
  That sun-burned man whose gods are twain,
Who kneels to Bridge from dark till day,
  And worships Golf till dusk again ;

Who finds the Devil kind enough,
  And knows no Hell but Social Scorn ;
Who likes a boy of pliant stuff,
  With all his instincts gently born,

And all his soul a shallow pool
  (Reflecting manufactured creeds)
Wherein the dreams that tempt a fool
  Are caught and drowned by kindly weeds ;

What would he turn and say to me,
  If looking in your serious eyes—
He saw strange ships across a sea
  Set sail for dim infinities ?

# TO THE FOOTBALL CAPTAIN

YOUR eyes have told me that your mind is clean,
  For through their sapphire casements I have seen
A great god-prefect (such as Heaven hath)
Watching that no small thought forget its bath.

And not a man on all the grimy earth
But envies you your god's complacent girth,
His Sandow biceps, and his sporting soul,
His swift and tricky dribbling into goal.

And yet when you have grown and come to years
Of ripened indiscretion, I have fears
Lest Mammon teach your thoughts to go untubbed,
And cast away the god who saw them scrubbed ;

Yet leave your emptied life to dribble round
From goal to goal across a footer ground,
Whereon the ghosts of strenuous hacks go by,
Kicking at nothing for eternity.

# TO A BOY WHO LAUGHED AT HIM

YOU found the uplands of my thought so flat
     That always when speech wandered from my
          mind
Your friendliness stood up and took its hat,
     And sauntered forth, and left a smile behind.

And first my self-sufficiency could float
     Above a light contempt so lightly born,
Until one day there caught me by the throat
     The sudden godhead of that very scorn.

For Poetry with her bare white feet,
     And laughing eyes by tears alit,
Walks sometimes in a miry street,
     But lives a million miles from it.

And while I searched her passing sign,
     And spoke of her as vulgars do,
She mourned the days when she was mine,
     And watched me through the eyes of—you.

You know her not.  She will move slow
     Along your sleeping staircase soon,
And lift a silent latch, and go
     Her way beneath the watching moon.

And you shall wake, nor find her gone,
     But work your work with eagerness,
And only when your toil is done
     Find it a moment somehow less.

And now when you have marked my style
   Within these lines of little worth,
Will dawn that faint, contemptuous smile
   Which bumps my music back to earth !

# HEAVEN

*(Found in his pocket after death.)*

SUDDENLY one day
The last ill shall fall away ;
The last little beastliness that is in our blood
Shall drop from us as the sheath drops from the bud,
And the great spirit of man shall struggle through,
And spread huge branches underneath the blue.
In any mirror, be it bright or dim,
Man will see God staring back at him.

# A LIST *of the* PUBLICATIONS
# OF THE
# POETRY BOOKSHOP

## ANTHOLOGIES

GEORGIAN POETRY, 1911-12. Edited by E. M. pp. 197. Brown Boards. *Twelfth Thousand.* Price 6s. net. (Postage 5d.).

GEORGIAN POETRY, 1913-15. Edited by E. M. pp. 244. Blue Boards. *Eleventh Thousand.* Price 6s. net. (Postage 5d.).

GEORGIAN POETRY, 1916-17. Edited by E. M. pp. 186. Green Boards. *Ninth Thousand.* Price 5s. net. (Postage 5d.).

ANTHOLOGY " DES IMAGISTES." Price 2s. 6d. net. (Postage 3d.).

A COLLECTION OF NURSERY RHYMES. *With one hundred decorations by C. Lovat Fraser.* 1s. net. Paper Boards, 1s. 6d. net. (Postage 1d.).

## CHAPBOOKS

THE OLD SHIPS. By JAMES ELROY FLECKER. *Third Thousand.* 1s. net.

SPRING MORNING. By FRANCES CORNFORD. *Second Thousand.* (Woodcuts by G. Raverat.) 1s. 3d. net.

THE FARMER'S BRIDE. By CHARLOTTE MEW. *Second Impression.* 1s. net.

STRANGE MEETINGS. By HAROLD MONRO. *Second Thousand.* 1s. net.

CHILDREN OF LOVE. By HAROLD MONRO. *Third Thousand.* 8d. net.

SINGSONGS OF THE WAR. By MAURICE HEWLETT. *Second Thousand.* 6d. net.

SONGS. By EDWARD SHANKS. *Second Impression.* 6d. net.

GOD SAVE THE KING. (A New Version.) By JAMES ELROY FLECKER. *Reprinted from* THE OLD SHIPS. 1d.

(Postage on each item, 1½d.).

No. 1. " Oh, what shall the Man ? " *Second Impression*. 3d. coloured. 2d. plain.

  ,,  2. Children's. *Second Impression*. 3d. coloured. 2d. plain.

  ,,  3. Poems by William Blake. Plain only. Price 1d.

  ,,  4. " Overheard on a Saltmarsh." (Harold Monro.) *Second Impression*. 3d. coloured. 2d. plain.

  ,,  5. " Arabia." (Walter De La Mare.) Coloured only. 3d.

  ,,  5. " Beautiful Meals." (T. Sturge Moore.) 3d. coloured. 2d. plain.

  ,,  7. " A Christmas Legend." (Frank Sidgwick.) 3d. coloured. 2d. plain.

  ,,  8. " The City." (John Drinkwater.) Coloured only. 3d.

  ,,  9. " Drinking." (Abraham Cowley.) 3d. coloured. 2d. plain.

  ,,  10. " Keith of Ravelston." (Bertram Dobell.) 3d. coloured. 2d. plain.

*The Decorations of No's. 1, 2, 4 and 5 are by Charles Winzer ; 6 by T. Sturge Moore ; 7 by Ethel Pye ; 8, 9 and 10 by C. Lovat Fraser.*

(Postage, up to 4 items, 1½d. ; the set of 10, 3d.).

# BROADSIDES

(Originally published by *The Flying Fame*.)

Price 4d. coloured ; 2d. plain.

A SONG. By Ralph Hodgson.
FEBRUARY. By Ralph Hodgson.
THE OLD MEN. By Walter De La Mare.
SUMMER. By C. Lovat Fraser.
STAFFORDSHIRE. By Oliver Davies.
THE BEGGAR. By Ralph Hodgson.
THE LATE LAST ROOK. By Ralph Hodgson.
THE BIRDCATCHER. By Ralph Hodgson.
THE BLIND FIDDLER'S DOG (Prose).

(Postage up to 15 items, 1½d.).

*All the decorations of the above are by C. Lovat Fraser.*

# GARLANDS

GARLAND OF PORTRAITURES. (4d. coloured; 2d. plain).

GARLAND OF NEW SONGS. By L. F. (6d. coloured; 4d. plain).

# BALLADS AND SONGS

SEVEN POEMS FROM BLAKE'S SONGS OF INNO-CENCE. (Decorated in Colours by G. SPENCER WATSON. Set to Music by GEOFFREY GWYTHER.) Price 9d. net each (postage ½d. each).

> No. I.—PIPING DOWN THE VALLEYS WILD.
> No. II.—THE SHEPHERD.
> No. III.—NURSE'S SONG.
> No. IV.—SPRING.
> No. V.—OPPORTUNITY.
> No. VI.—INFANT JOY.
> No. VII.—NIGHT.

Set complete in Decorated Portfolio, 6s. 6d. net (Postage 3d.)

A BALLAD OF "THE GLOSTER" AND "THE GOEBEN." By MAURICE HEWLETT. *Fifth Thousand.* Coloured. Price 2d. (postage ½d.).

THE KING'S HIGHWAY. By HENRY NEWBOLT. Music by Francis Newbolt. *Third Thousand.* Coloured. Price 3d. (postage ½d.).

# MISCELLANEOUS

DEIRDRE AND OTHER DRAMAS. By MICHAEL FIELD. Yellow Wrappers. 5s. net (postage 3d.).

POEMS. By JOHN ALFORD. Price 2s. net (postage 2d.).

POETRY AND DRAMA, 1913 and 1914. Bound in Brown Paper Boards, Buckram Back, with Index and Title-Page. Two Volumes, four numbers in each. 12s. 6d. each net. Separate Numbers are still obtainable at 2s. 6d. net each (postage 3d.).

CADENCES. By F. S. Flint.

IMAGES. By Richard Aldington.

OVER THE BRAZIER. By Robert Graves.

THE CONTEMPLATIVE QUARRY. By Anna Wickham.

FIVE NEW POEMS. By James Stephens.

ANTWERP. By Ford Madox Hueffer.

THE MYSTERY. By Ralph Hodgson.

THE BULL. By Ralph Hodgson. (*Reprinted in Georgian Poetry*, 1913-15).

THE SONG OF HONOUR. By Ralph Hodgson. (*Reprinted in Georgian Poetry*, 1913-15).

EVE. By Ralph Hodgson.

EIGHT NEW POEMS. By W. B. Yeats.

TREES. By Harold Monro. (*Reprinted in Strange Meetings*).

*Broadsides* :—THE ROBIN'S SONG. THE WIND. THE GIPSY GIRL.

Full Particulars of the Bookshop, together with details of the Readings of Poetry given there, and Catalogues, may be had post free on application.